W9-AOW-662

DAVY'S DREAM

Written and Illustrated
by
PAUL OWEN LEWIS

Whitecap Books
Vancouver/Toronto

Text and illustrations copyright © 1988 by Paul Owen Lewis

Whitecap Books
Vancouver / Toronto

First published by Beyond Words Publishing, Inc., Hillsboro, Oregon. All rights reserved.

Canadian edition 1999

All rights reserved. No part of this book may be reproduced, stored in a retrieval system, or transmitted in any form by any means, electronic, mechanical, photocopying, recording or otherwise, without prior written permission of Tricycle Press, P.O. Box 7123, Berkeley, California 94707. For information on this or other Whitecap titles, please write to Whitecap Books Ltd., 351 Lynn Avenue, North Vancouver, BC V7J 2C4.

Printed in Hong Kong

Canadian Cataloguing in Publication Data

Lewis, Paul Owen.
    Davy's dream

    ISBN 1-55110-926-3

    1. Killer whale—Juvenile fiction. I. Title.
PZ7.L48Da 1999   j813'.54   C99-910102-1

Also by Paul Owen Lewis:
Frog Girl
Grasper
P. Bear's New Year's Party
Storm Boy

Dedicated to the memory of my friend and father,
GARY BARTON LEWIS.
With thanks to Jasper,
Mimi, and C.B. Johnston.

One sunny afternoon,
a boy named Davy
lay in the tall grass
on a hilltop dreaming.

It was a dream of killer whales.

He saw himself sailing among them

in play,

in song,

in silence,

and in joy.

When he awoke,
he ran down the hill into the harbor town
eager to share his dream of the happy whales
with the people there.

"Ha, wild Orca? They're dangerous," laughed an old fisherman.

"Not like those tame ones doin' tricks."

"Yep, 'Wolves of the Sea' we call 'em around here," agreed another.

"Hunt in packs and eat anything," said yet another, squinting his eyes as he spoke.

Davy suddenly felt very foolish. He told no one else about his dream that day.

But the wonder he felt for the whales
and the memory of the dream
would not leave him.
He sailed out of the harbor
and into the straits
to look for them.

Not long afterwards,
far away on the water's surface,
he saw what looked like little black triangles.

Killer whale fins!

Quickly he trimmed the sails
and raced towards them.
Davy's hopes rose together with the
spray off the bow of the boat.
But, he could soon tell, the whales were
swimming away from him faster than
he could follow.

Once more he trimmed the sails.
Davy's hopes rose
as he raced towards them.
But at the last moment,
the whales dived — and vanished.

He tried again and again,
  but always it seemed the whales
  would have nothing to do
  with the boy in the boat.
  "I guess the dream
    was just a dream after all,"
  Davy said to himself.
  He sailed for home.

The next day,
      Davy was bored and restless.
         With nothing better to do
      he climbed back up
   his sunny hilltop to think.
As he sat,
      the heat of the sun made him drowsy.
         He lay down in the grass,
            closed his eyes,
            fell asleep,
      and began
to dream again . . .

When he awoke,
he ran down into the town —
and telling no one . . .

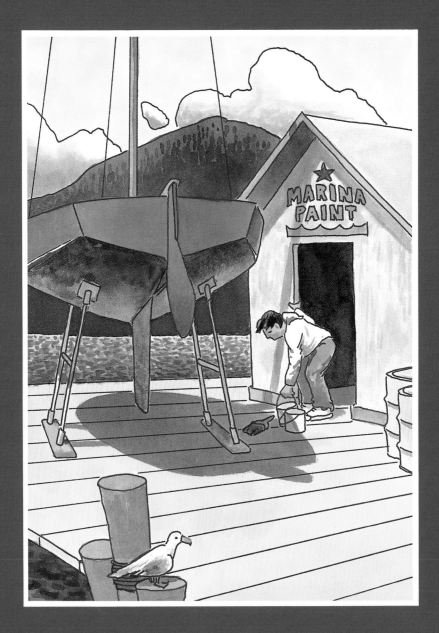

Playing, singing, resting,
and jumping for joy together —
Davy and his new friends had done it all!
But now, the setting sun reminded him that it
would soon be dark. It was time to go home.
Davy waved goodbye,
and the whales each spouted in reply.

The evening air darkened quickly as the little
sailboat glided home alone. Then, without
warning, there was a loud

CRUNCH

and the boat lurched to a stop.
Davy knew at once he must have hit a rock
as water began to fill the boat.
The boat was sinking.

No sooner had he started bailing
when two towering black fins
rose out of the water
on either side of the boat.
The boat began to rise —
and move forward very fast.

In no time at all
Davy was safely back in the harbor.

The next morning, Davy told everything to the fishermen.

"Boy," said the first, "you've been watching too much TV!"

"Imagine that," said the second, "being rescued by wild killer whales. That lad can sure tell a good fish story!"

"Got a screw loose more likely," said the third, squinting his eyes as he spoke.

Davy left the men again.
But this time, a great big smile grew on his face.
Because he knew — and you and I know too —
that dreams can come true.

Centerville Library
Washington-Centerville Public Library
Centerville, Ohio
DISCARD

W9-AFM-719

I, VAMPIRE

VOLUME 1 **TAINTED LOVE**

I, VAMPIRE

VOLUME 1
TAINTED LOVE

JOSHUA HALE **FIALKOV** writer

ANDREA **SORRENTINO** artist

MARCELO **MAIOLO** colorist

PAT **BROSSEAU** letterer

MATT IDELSON Editor – Original Series WIL MOSS Associate Editor – Original Series
ROWENA YOW Editor ROBBIN BROSTERMAN Design Director – Books ROBBIE BIEDERMAN Publication Design

BOB HARRAS VP – Editor-In-Chief

DIANE NELSON President DAN DIDIO and JIM LEE Co-Publishers GEOFF JOHNS Chief Creative Officer
JOHN ROOD Executive VP – Sales, Marketing and Business Development AMY GENKINS Senior VP – Business and Legal Affairs
NAIRI GARDINER Senior VP – Finance JEFF BOISON VP – Publishing Operations
MARK CHIARELLO VP – Art Direction and Design JOHN CUNNINGHAM VP – Marketing
TERRI CUNNINGHAM VP – Talent Relations and Services ALISON GILL Senior VP – Manufacturing and Operations
HANK KANALZ Senior VP – Digital JAY KOGAN VP – Business and Legal Affairs, Publishing JACK MAHAN VP – Business Affairs, Talent
NICK NAPOLITANO VP – Manufacturing Administration SUE POHJA VP – Book Sales
COURTNEY SIMMONS Senior VP – Publicity BOB WAYNE Senior VP – Sales

I, VAMPIRE VOLUME 1: TAINTED LOVE

Published by DC Comics. Cover and compilation Copyright © 2012 DC Comics. All Rights Reserved.

Originally published in single magazine form in I, VAMPIRE #1-6. Copyright © 2011, 2012 DC Comics. All Rights Reserved. All characters, their distinctive likenesses and related elements featured in this publication are trademarks of DC Comics. The stories, characters and incidents featured in this publication are entirely fictional. DC Comics does not read or accept unsolicited ideas, stories or artwork.

DC Comics, 1700 Broadway, New York, NY 10019
A Warner Bros. Entertainment Company.
Printed by RR Donnelley, Salem, VA, USA. 8/31/12. First Printing.

ISBN: 978-1-4012-3687-8

Library of Congress Cataloging-in-Publication Data

Fialkov, Joshua Hale, 1979-
I, Vampire volume 1 : tainted love / Joshua Hale Fialkov, Andrea Sorrentino.
p. cm.
"Originally published in single magazine form in I, Vampire 1-6."
ISBN 978-1-4012-3687-8
1. Graphic novels. I. Sorrentino, Andrea. II. Title.
PN6728.I23F53 2012
741.5'973—dc23
                    2012022440

 SUSTAINABLE Certified Chain of Custody

cover art by
JENNY FRISON

"MARY. WHAT I DID TO YOU WAS WRONG. I'VE DONE NOTHING BUT TRY TO UNDO IT--"

"BUT I'M HAPPY, ANDREW. DON'T YOU GET THAT?"

"HAPPY? MARY. YOU'RE EVIL."

WH- WHERE AM I?

YOU'RE...

THERE WAS AN ATTACK--

YOU DIDN'T MAKE IT.

GOD, YOU LOOK JUST LIKE HER.

BUT HOW--

OH GOD...

MY SKIN IS BURNING...

GET OFF!

"JUST ONE NIGHT. ONE LAST CHANCE FOR US TO BE TOGETHER LIKE WE WERE.

"BEFORE."

"WE CAN'T EVER GO BACK, MARY. NOT UNTIL I FIND A WAY TO CURE YOU--"

"CURE ME OF WHAT?!?"

"I LOVE YOU, ANDREW. AND I'M SORRY."

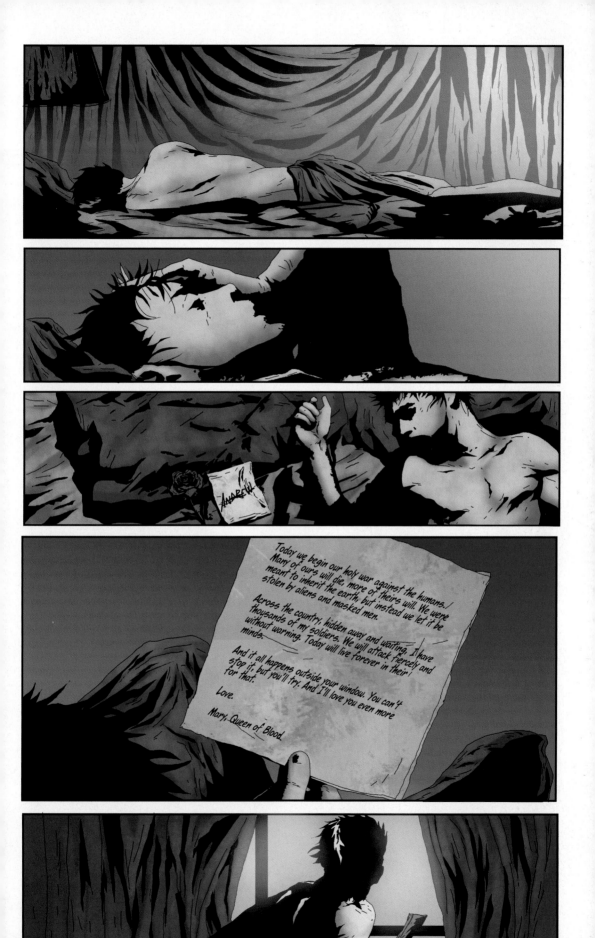

cover art by
JENNY FRISON

SHOWTIME.

TWENTY-FIVE MINUTES AGO.

QUIET! QUIET!

SHUT YOUR MOUTHS!

QUIET, CHILDREN.

YOUR BIG BROTHER WANTS TO SPEAK.

I...UH... THANK YOU, MA'AM.

WE...MY FRIENDS, WE ARE THE CHOSEN!

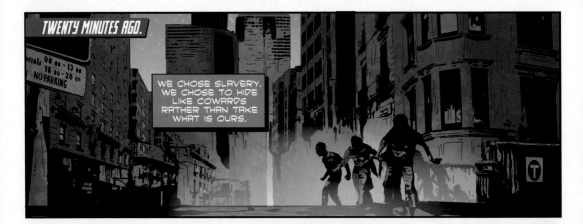

TWENTY MINUTES AGO.

WE CHOSE SLAVERY. WE CHOSE TO HIDE LIKE COWARDS RATHER THAN TAKE WHAT IS OURS.

I DO NOT FEAR WHAT I AM.

I DO NOT FEAR DEATH.

AND I SURE AS HELL DO NOT FEAR AN EARTH WITHOUT *THEM* ON IT.

FIVE MINUTES AGO.

I HAVE SEEN THE FUTURE, AND IT IS AN AMAZING WORLD WHERE THE RIVERS RUN RED WITH BLOOD AND THE SUN HAS BEEN BLOTTED OUT.

BUT I DREAM OF A LIFE WHERE THE ONE BEING ON EARTH WHO GIVES ME A FEELING OTHER THAN HUNGER OR HATRED WANTS NOTHING MORE THAN TO BE BY MY SIDE.

TODAY IS THE FIRST DAY OF A NEW ERA.

TODAY IS THE END OF DECADES OF HIDING IN TERROR, STRUGGLING TO FIND OUR PLACE.

TODAY IS THE GREATEST DAY IN THE WORLD.

cover art by
JENNY FRISON

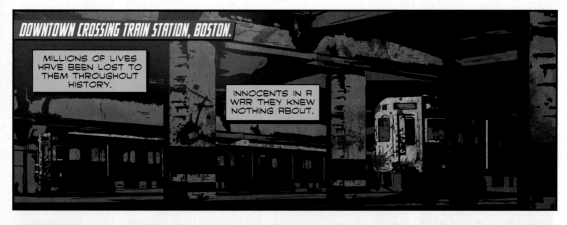

DOWNTOWN CROSSING TRAIN STATION, BOSTON.

MILLIONS OF LIVES HAVE BEEN LOST TO THEM THROUGHOUT HISTORY.

INNOCENTS IN A WAR THEY KNEW NOTHING ABOUT.

PLY, SMITH, AND COHEN STOCK BROKERS, STAR CITY.

BUT ASIDE FROM A STRAY HERE AND THERE, THAT STOPPED FIVE YEARS AGO.

THERE WAS PEACE.

TASTE OF HEAVEN DONUT SHOP, COAST CITY.

THE THING THAT EVERYONE KNOWS TO BE TRUE AND YET SECRETLY HOPES IS A LIE...

PEACE IS FLEETING.

APOLLO'S LANDING NIGHTCLUB, LOS ANGELES.

THE NEEDS OF THE INDIVIDUAL WILL CONFLICT WITH THE NEEDS OF THE MANY--

AND THE NEEDS OF THE MINORITY WILL ATTACK THE NEEDS OF THE MAJORITY--

IN THE NEAR THIRTY-FIVE YEARS I'VE KNOWN HIM, I'VE NEVER SEEN ANDREW HURT. NOT LIKE THIS.

NO MATTER WHAT HE'S FACED WITH, HE'S ALWAYS WON.

I PRAY THAT WILL ALWAYS BE THE CASE.

BUCHANAN ARMS APARTMENTS, SAN FRANCISCO, 1979.

HOW MANY HAVE YOU MASSACRED?

HUNDREDS! THEY COME TO US LIKE FLIES TO HONEY!

THAT FIRST NIGHT I MET HIM, HE SEEMED LIKE SOMETHING OUT OF A VICTORIAN NOVEL...

BUT HE WAS SO MUCH MORE EVEN THEN.

YOU PROMISE THEM SEX AND DRUGS, AND INSTEAD YOU FEED ON THEM!

NO! WE EAT THEM AFTER.

THE HIGH IS AMAZING!

COME TO ME!

BACK! BACK, I SAY!

I SPENT MY ENTIRE LIFE LEARNING TO HATE VAMPIRES.

WHAT THEY STAND FOR, WHAT THEY DO, HOW THEY LIVE.

BUT SOMEHOW, THIS MAN RADIATES... GOOD.

WHEN I MET HIM, I KNEW THAT I'D FIGHT AT HIS SIDE TILL THE DAY I DIED.

HOLD ON.

HERE.

I DIDN'T THINK ABOUT WHAT I WAS GIVING UP, BECAUSE I KNEW WHAT HE SACRIFICED TO BECOME WHAT HE IS.

BE CAREFUL AND KEEP QUIET.

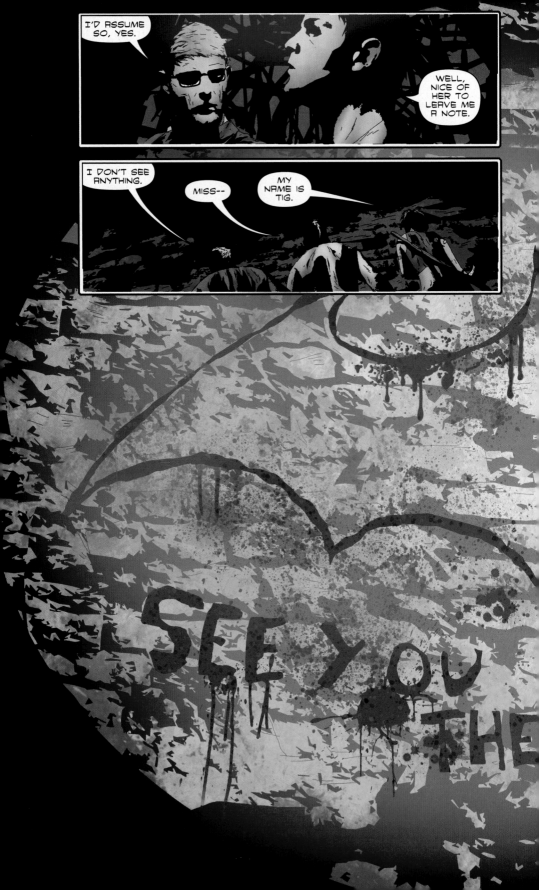

WE'RE NOT THE FIRST STRAYS ANDREW PICKED UP.

HE DRAWS PEOPLE TO HIM. IT'S A GIFT.

ALTHOUGH OBVIOUSLY THAT SWAY IS ONE OF HIS POWERS.

THIS GIRL WANTED TO KILL HIM FIVE MINUTES AGO, NOW SHE WANTS TO GO ON A ROAD TRIP WITH HIM.

I LEARNED A LOT ABOUT HIS KIND OVER THE THIRTY-PLUS YEARS I'VE BEEN WITH HIM.

HOW THEY LIVE. HOW THEY DIE.

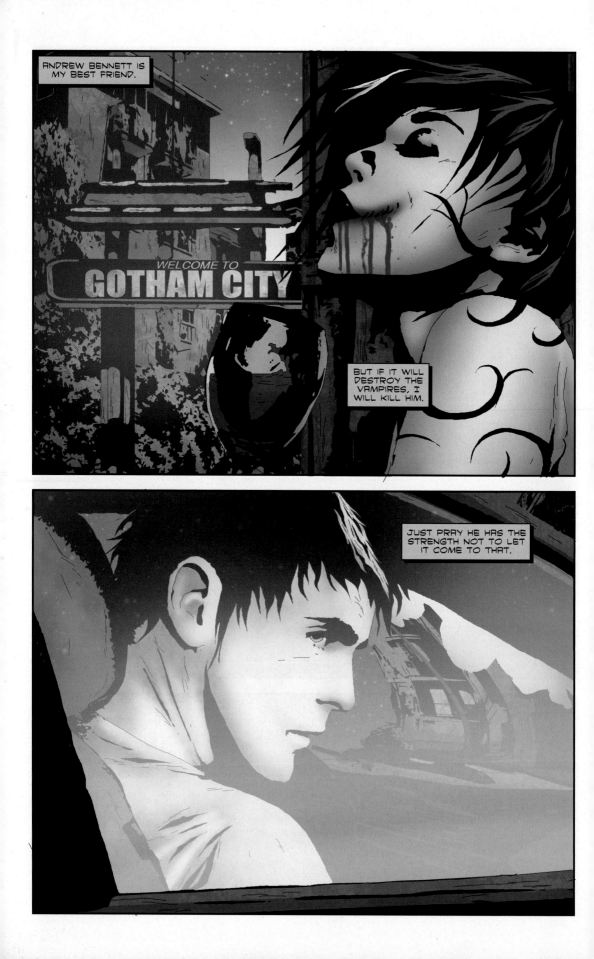

cover art by
JENNY FRISON

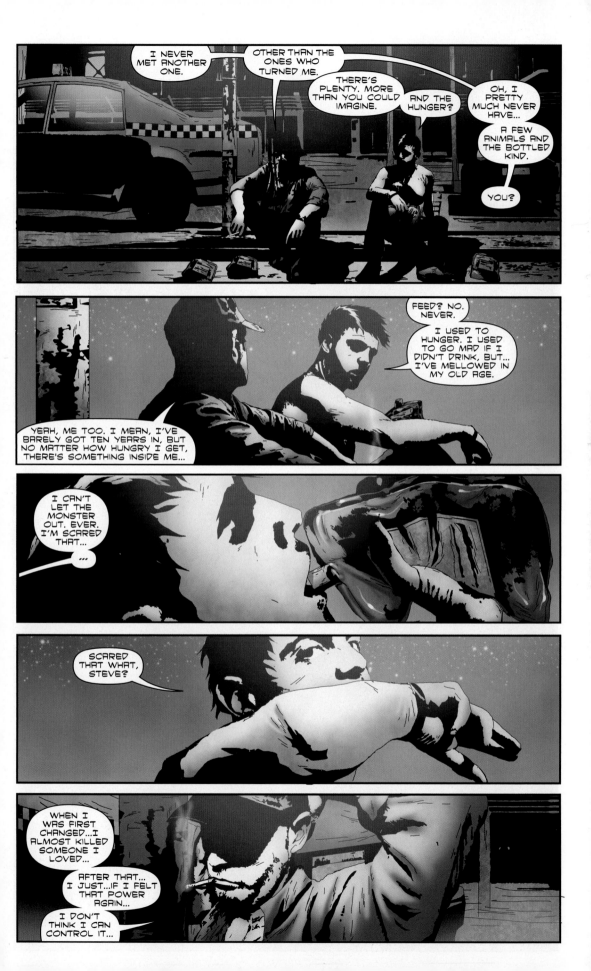

YOU CAN'T DO THAT IN HERE, SON.

CAN'T DO WHAT, LOVE?

SMOKE. AIN'T ALLOWED IN RESTAURANTS.

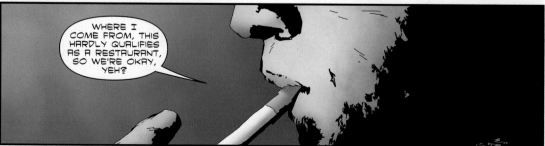

WHERE I COME FROM, THIS HARDLY QUALIFIES AS A RESTAURANT, SO WE'RE OKAY, YEH?

BANG!

WHAT THE HELL?

cover art by
JENNY FRISON

cover art by
ANDREA SORRENTINO & MARCELO MAIOLO

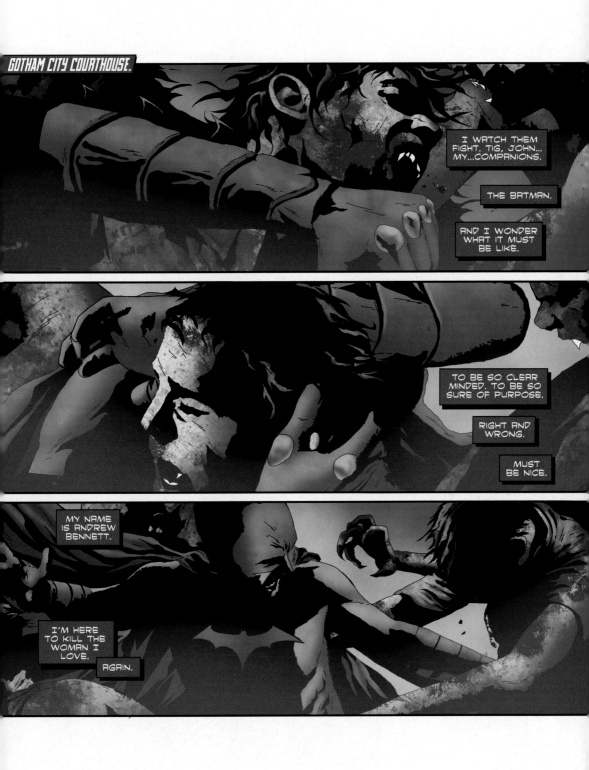

PURPOSE. A REASON TO LIVE.

JUST MY LUCK THAT WHEN I'M SITTING HERE WITH A SWORD THROUGH MY HEART COURTESY OF A CRAZED TEENAGE GIRL, I'D FIGURE IT OUT.

THAT NOW, FACING MARY, WITH MY HEAD CUT OFF, FEELING THE SECONDS TICK AWAY, I'D KNOW.

I'M NOT HERE TO STOP MARY.

MY PURPOSE IS TO WIPE ALL VAMPIRES OFF THE FACE OF THE PLANET.

MY PURPOSE IS TO MAKE THE WORLD A SAFE PLACE--

--AND ERADICATE A PLAGUE THAT I'M AT LEAST SEMI-RESPONSIBLE FOR SPREADING.